MARIE PEACEY

CAPE TOWN

Dedicated to my husband, Basil Peacey and to my daughters, Carina, Annabeth and Janeke Peacey.

A special word of thanks to my mother, Johanna van Eeden, and to Rita Vermeulen for their assistance and to Annabeth Peacey for tracing my designs.

© 1990 Delos
40 Heerengracht, Cape Town

Also available in Afrikaans as **Knip dit Weg**

Photography by David Briers, Kevin Taylor, Eric Stephenson and Charles Corbett
Illustrations by Marie Peacey
Models: Jaycee de Reuck, Carina Peacey and Liz Tonks
Typography and cover design by Lou and Joy Wrench
Typeset in 10 on 12 pt Clearface Regular & Helvetica
Printed and bound by Blackshaws, Cape Town

First edition, first impression 1990

ISBN 1-86826-134-4

Contents

Photo 1: Cut-away
decoration on pockets
(Marianne van Dyk)

Photo 2: Cut-away
decoration on a blouse
(Santjie Marais)

Cut-away (also known as reverse appliqué)

Cut-away patterns are achieved by stacking together two or more layers of material of different colours or different tones of the same colour and cutting away areas from the top layer, and then the layers beneath, to reveal each successive colour. One does not have to be artistic to achieve an interesting effect, because with only a few rectangles and circles, as seen on the pocket in Photo 1, one can create an artistic decoration. Plain colours can be combined with printed material as seen on the blouse in Photo 2. The designs for the cut-away decorations on the pockets and the blouse appear on p. 30.

Cut-away in mola

Mola is a type of needlecraft practised by Cuna Indian women from the San Blas Islands, which are situated off the Panama coast, and it is used to decorate their clothing. The Cuna craftswomen use powerful colours with lots of red, black, orange, yellow, blue and green cotton material. A traditional mola, using only the cut-away technique is easy to recognise because of the narrow channels, dots and sawtooth lines that fill every available space. The yoke illustrated in Photo 3 is an example of this work. Seven layers of different colours were used together here.

One can put many layers of material on top of one another, but one must remember that the "islands" have to be big enough to reveal all the bottom layers when the top ones are cut away. The design appears on p. 31.

Photo 3: Mola decoration on a blouse (Marie Peacey)

Basic instructions

Materials

- Two or more layers of pure cotton material
- Matching thread
- Embroidery scissors
- Thin needle
- Dressmaker's carbon paper
- Pins
- Design
- Ballpoint pen
- Marking pencil

Method

1. Tack the two or more layers of material together along the outer edges.

2. Place the dressmaker's carbon paper with the coloured side face down on the top layer of material. Put the design on top of the carbon and pin the design, carbon and material together. Trace the design onto the material with the ballpoint pen.

3. Remove the design and carbon paper.

4. The design consists of small islands. Tack the layers of material together between the islands 5 mm on the outside of the design lines.

5. Cut the islands out by piercing the top layer of the material with the point of the embroidery scissors and cutting 5 mm on the inside of the design lines. Cut only the top layer. Make incisions where necessary (Figs. 1–8).

6. Fold the cut edges of the material under with the tip of the needle (Fig. 9) and stitch them down onto the next layer with small hemming stitches.

7. Where there are more than two layers of material, draw a line 3 mm from the previous folded line with a marking pencil, cut 5 mm from this marked line, fold the edges under and sew down with small hemming stitches. Continue like this until the last layer of material is revealed.

8. Remove tacking stitches.

Fig. 1

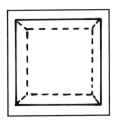

Fig. 2

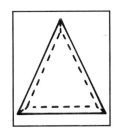

Fig. 3

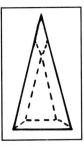

Fig. 4

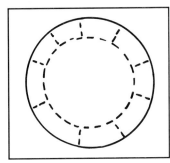

Fig. 5

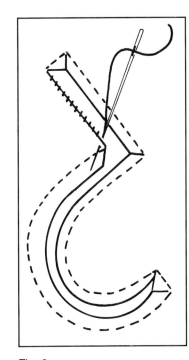

Fig. 6

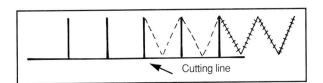

Cutting line

Fig. 7: Sawtooth line

Fig. 8

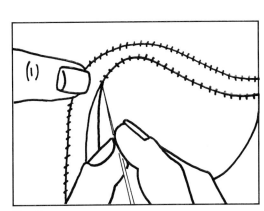

(1)

Fig. 9

7

Photo 4: Pa ndau

Materials

- Two layers of material – top layer in pure white cotton
- Matching thread
- Embroidery scissors
- Thin needle
- Dressmaker's carbon paper
- Pins
- Ballpoint pen
- Design (see photo 4)

Method

1. Tack the two layers of material together along the outer edges.

2. Place the dressmaker's carbon paper, with the coloured side face down, on the top layer of the material. Put the design on top of the carbon and pin the design, carbon and material together. Trace the design onto the material with the ballpoint pen.

3. Remove the design and carbon paper.

4. The design consists of thin channels. Tack on both sides of the channels.

5. Pierce the top layer of the material with the point of the embroidery scissors and cut down the middle of the space between the lines (Fig. 6).

6. Fold the edges of the material under with the tip of the needle (Fig. 9) and stitch them down onto the second layer with small hemming stitches.

7. Remove the tacking stitches (Photo 4).

The same technique was used as for the Pa ndau, with pieces of grey material appliquéd into position on the bigger background areas (Photo 5). The design appears on p. 32.

Photo 5: Black-and-white birds (Rita Vermeulen)

Black-and-white birds

Method

1. Follow instructions 1–6 for Pa ndau.

2. Draw a line on the white material approximately 3 mm from the folded edge.

3. Cut 5 mm outside the line, fold the edges under with the tip of the needle and stitch them down onto the third layer of material with small hemming stitches thus revealing large black areas.

4. Appliqué pieces of grey material on the larger white areas.

Photo 6: Hawaiian appliqué
(Rita Vermeulen)

Materials

- Two layers of material in strongly contrasting colours – top layer of pure cotton fabric

- Matching thread

- Embroidery scissors

- Marking pencil

- Paper scissors

- Paper

- Thin needle

- This method enables one to appliqué very thin or complicated pieces of material onto the bottom layer of fabric

Method

1. Fold a square piece of paper in half, then fold it in half again (Fig. 10).

2. Draw a design on the outer surface of the folded square as shown in Fig. 11 and cut along the line.

3. Open up the folded paper and flatten it onto a piece of material, pin into position, and trace along the outline of the paper shape with a marking pencil.

4. Remove the paper and tack this material onto another piece of material of contrasting colour. Tack along the outer edges and 6 mm on the inside of the marked line (Fig. 12).

5. Cut away the top layer of material about 6 mm on the outside of the marked line.

6. Cut small incisions where necessary (Figs. 1–7).

7. Fold the cut edge under itself along the marked line and sew onto the bottom layer of material with small hemming stitches (Photo 6).

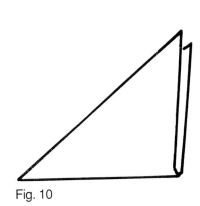

Fig. 10

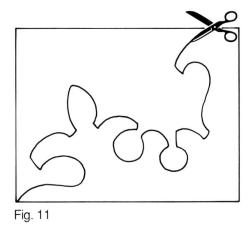

Fig. 11

Fig. 12

Photo 7: Thin-line appliqué
(Rita Vermeulen)

Materials

- Two layers of material
- Matching thread
- Embroidery scissors
- Thin needle
- Dressmaker's carbon paper
- Pins
- Design (see p. 33)

Method

1. Tack the two or more layers of material together along the outer edges.

2. Place the dressmaker's carbon paper with the coloured side face down on the top layer of material. Put the design on top of the carbon and pin the design, carbon and material together. Trace the design onto the material with the ballpoint pen.

3. Remove the design and carbon paper.

4. The design consists of small islands. Tack in the middle of the channels around the islands.

5. Cut the islands out by piercing the top layer of the material with the point of the embroidery scissors and cutting 5 mm on the inside of the design lines. Cut only the top layer. Make incisions where necessary (Figs. 1–8).

6. Fold the cut edges of the material under with the tip of the needle (Fig. 9) and stitch them down onto the next layer with small hemming stitches.

7. Remove tacking stitches (Photo 7).

Photo 8: Basque
for harem pants

Basque for harem pants

Materials

- Three layers of material in different tones of the same colour
- Matching thread
- Embroidery scissors
- Thin needle
- Dressmaker's carbon paper
- Pins
- Design (see p. 34)

Method

1. Tack the two or three layers of material together along the outer edges.

2. Place the dressmaker's carbon paper with the coloured side face down on the top layer of material. Put the design on top of the carbon and pin the design, carbon and material together. Trace the design onto the material with the ballpoint pen.

3. Remove the design and carbon paper.

4. The design consists of small islands. Tack the layers of material together between the islands 5 mm on the outside of the design lines.

5. Cut the islands out by piercing the top layer of the material with the point of the embroidery scissors and cutting 5 mm on the inside of the design lines. Cut only the top layer. Make incisions where necessary (Figs. 1–8).

6. Fold the cut edges of the material under with the tip of the needle (Fig. 9) and stitch them down onto the next layer with small hemming stitches.

7. Where there are more than two layers of material, draw a line 3 mm from the previous folded line with a marking pencil, cut 5 mm from this marked line, fold the edges under and sew down with small hemming stitches. Continue like this until the last layer of material is revealed.

8. Remove tacking stitches (Photo 8).

Photo 9: Braces with cut-away decoration
(Marie Peacey)

Braces

Materials

- Two layers of plain coloured material and several smaller pieces of material of different colours
- Matching thread
- Embroidery scissors
- Thin needle
- Dressmaker's carbon paper
- Marking pencil
- Pins
- Bias binding
- Design (see p. 35)

Method

1. Tack two layers of material together along the outer edges.

2. Place the dressmaker's carbon paper with the coloured side face down on the top layer of material. Put the design on top of the carbon and pin the design, carbon and material together. Trace the design onto the material with the ballpoint pen.

3. Remove the design and carbon paper.

4. The design consists of small islands. Tack the layers of material together between the islands 5 mm on the outside of the design lines.

5. Cut the islands out by piercing the top layer of the material with the point of the embroidery scissors and cutting 5 mm on the inside of the design lines. Cut only the top layer. Make incisions where necessary (Figs. 1–8).

6. Fold the cut edges of the material under with the tip of the needle (Fig. 9) and stitch them down onto the next layer with small hemming stitches.

7. Tack smaller pieces of material behind the second layer of material.

8. Where there are more than two layers of material, draw a line 3 mm from the previous folded line with a marking pencil, cut 5 mm from this marked line, fold the edges under and sew down with small hemming stitches. Continue like this until the last layer of material is revealed.

9. Remove tacking stitches.

10. Finish off with bias binding (Photo 9).

Tea cosy

Different pieces of German print material were used for the third layer (Photo 10). The design appears on p. 36.

Photo 10: Tea cosy
(Rita Vermeulen)

Purple waistcoat

Two different coloured strips of material were used for the third layer (Photo 11). The design appears on p. 37.

Photo 11: Purple waistcoat
(Marie Peacey)

Jacket

The colours for the cut-away work were chosen to match the colours in the roughly-woven material of the jacket. The bird was embroidered with brightly-coloured embroidery thread (Photo 12). The design appears on p. 38.

Photo 12: Jacket with cut-away decoration and embroidery (Ann Strauss)

Black T-shirt

Different pieces of printed material were used for the fourth layer (Photo 13). Follow instructions as for the three-layer cut-away, but add a fourth layer by tacking small pieces of printed material in position under the third layer. The design appears on p. 39.

Photo 13: Decorated black T-shirt (Rita Vermeulen)

Black jacket with cut-away collar

Only plain colours were used for this collar (Photo 14). The design appears on p. 40.

Photo 14: Black jacket with cut-away collar (Rita Vermeulen)

Photo 15: Mandala
(Pam Potgieter)

Mandala

Materials

- Two layers of pure cotton material in different colours (e.g. royal blue and purple)
- Three smaller squares of cotton material (e.g. green, pink and cream)
- Matching thread
- Embroidery scissors
- Thin needle
- Dressmaker's carbon paper
- Pins
- Design (see p. 19)

Method

1. Tack the royal blue and purple layers of material together along the outer edges.

2. Trace the design onto the top purple layer of material.

3. Tack in the middle of each circle (Fig. 13).

4. Cut 5 mm on the outside of the design line, but only through the top layer of material.

5. Fold the cut edges under and sew down on the bottom layer with small hemming stitches. Only the purple circles remain on top of the royal blue layer.

6. Trace the middle square of the design onto green material and cut out the square - allow 5 mm hem allowance all round.

7. Tack into position (Fig. 14).

8. Sew in position with small hemming stitches.

9. Cut out the five shapes on the square and hem them down as well.

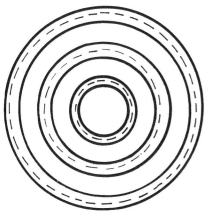

Fig. 13

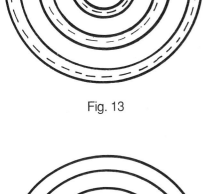

Fig. 14

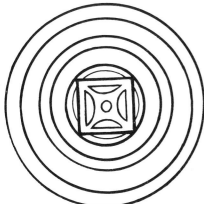

Fig. 15

10. Trace the second square of the design onto pink material (Fig. 15).

11. Cut out the middle section of the square and tack over the next square.

12. Sew in position with small hemming stitches.

13. Cut out the rest of the shapes on the square, fold the cut edges under and sew down with small hemming stitches.

14. Trace the third square (Fig. 16).

15. Cut out the middle section of the square and tack into the correct position over the previous shapes.

16. Fold the cut edges under and sew down with small hemming stitches.

17. The broad outer line of the pink square and the cream squares can be broken up by cutting a slit in the middle. Fold the cut edges under and sew down with small hemming stitches (Photo 15).

Fig. 16

Photo 16: Belt
(Rita Vermeulen)

Belt
The same technique is used as with the Mandala

Materials

- Yellow, purple, pink and green material
- Matching thread
- Embroidery scissors
- Thin needle
- Dressmaker's carbon paper
- Pins
- Bias binding
- Beads
- Design (see p. 40)

Method

1. Cut out the shape of the belt in yellow, purple, pink, and green material.

2. Trace the design onto the purple material.

3. Tack the purple material onto the yellow material along the outer edges as well as around the islands, about 5 mm from the design line.

4. Cut out the shapes, 5 mm on the inside of the design line.

5. Fold the edges under and sew down.

6. Trace the same design onto the pink material, but move the design about 2 cm to the right before tracing.

7. Tack the pink layer of material onto the first two layers, cut out and sew as above. The shapes which are exposed are now slightly off-centre.

8. Trace the same design onto the green material, but again move the design 2 cm to the right before tracing.

9. Tack the green layer of material onto the first three layers, cut out and sew as above.

10. Finish the belt off with bias binding and beads as shown on Photo 16.

Photo 17: White face
(Rita Vermeulen)

White face

Materials

- Seven layers of white cotton material
- Matching thread
- Embroidery scissors
- Thin needle
- Dressmaker's carbon paper
- Pins
- Marking pencil
- Design (see p. 41)

Method

1. Tack seven layers of material together along the outer edges.

2. Trace the design onto the top layer of material.

3. Tack the inside of the islands about 5 mm from the design line.

4. Cut through only the top layer of material about 5 mm from the outside of the design line.

5. Fold the cut edges of the material under with the tip of the needle and stitch them down onto the next layer of material with small hemming stitches.

6. Draw a line 3 mm from the previous folded line with a marking pencil. Cut 5 mm from this marked line through the next layer of material, fold the edges under and sew down with small hemming stitches.

7. Continue like this until the last layer of material is exposed. Remember to cut into the next layer of material only where it is possible to fold the edges under and still have a remaining edge left.

8. Remove the tacking stitches (Photo 17).

Photo 18: Cut-away on a knitted garment
(Marie Peacey)

Decorated jersey

Materials

- Iron-on interlining or paper
- Pencil
- Design (see p. 42)
- Scissors
- Darning needle
- Elle wool: Kiddies Kuddle, Frolic 4-ply, Frolic Industrial

Method

1. Knit the jersey either by hand or on a knitting machine. Finish the neck neatly with a ribbing.

2. Sew the shoulder seams together and join the sleeves to the jersey on the inside.

3. Trace the design onto iron-on interlining or paper.

4. Knit pieces large enough for the design pieces on a knitting machine.

5. Press the knitted pieces lightly with a steam iron.

6. Pin the interlining or paper designs onto the knitted pieces, adding 1 cm hem allowance around each and cut them out.

7. Remove the design from the knitted pieces.

8. Pin the knitted pieces in position on the jersey, fold the edges under 1 cm and tack.

9. Use matching wool and sew the edge down with small hemming stitches close together so that each knitted stitch is sewn down.

10. Tack a red circle into position over a smaller black circle on the jersey.

11. Fold the edge under and sew the circle down with small hemming stitches.

12. Cut away the centre piece of the red circle so that the black circle underneath is revealed.

13. Fold the cut edges under and sew down.

14. Cut away the centre piece of the black circle so that the jersey is revealed underneath.

15. Fold the edges under and sew down with small hemming stitches.

16. Cut a channel in the big red area to reveal the white piece underneath.

17. Fold the cut edges under and sew down with small hemming stitches.

18. Embroider with stem stitch, fly stitch and French knots (Figs. 17, 18 and 19).

19. Complete the jersey by sewing up the underarm and side seams on the inside of the garment (Photo 18).

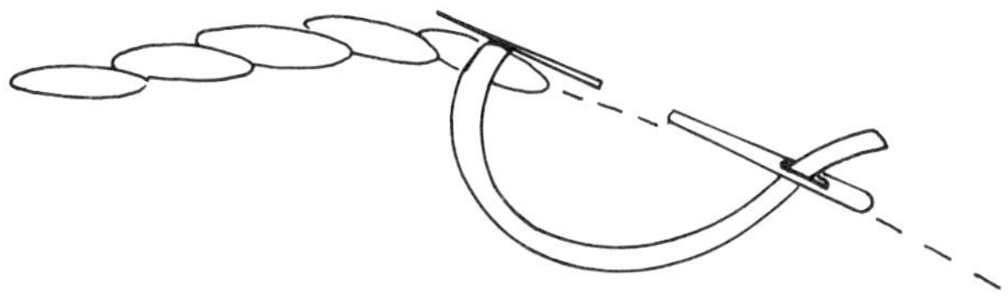

Fig. 17: Stem stitch

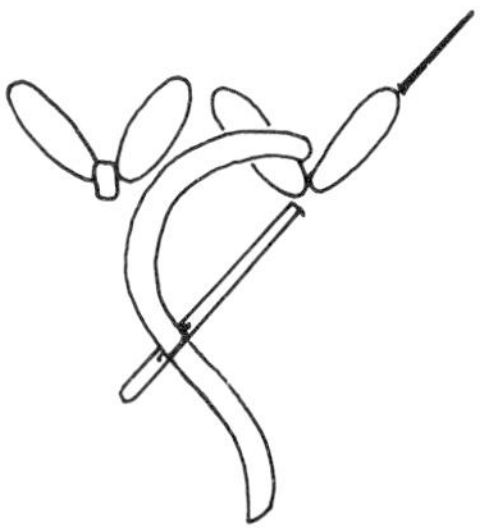

Fig. 18: Fly stitch

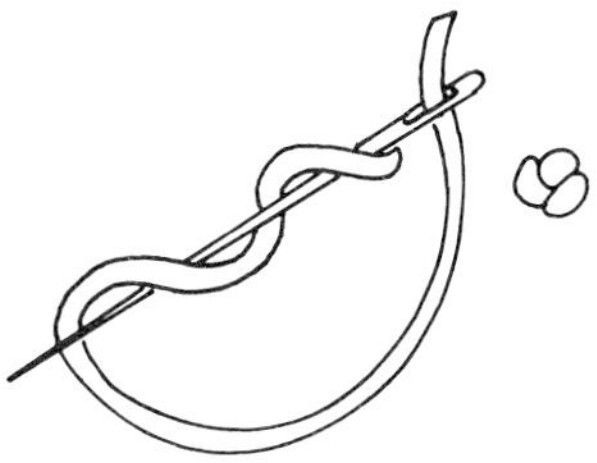

Fig. 19: French knot

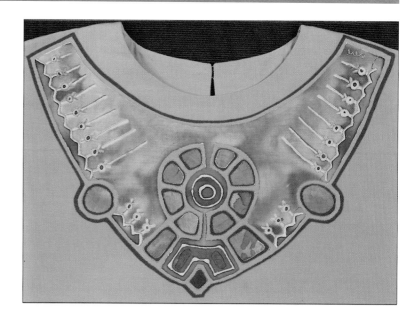

Photo 19: Cut-away
decoration on a dress
(Elsie Smith)

Dress

Materials

- Two layers of material: top
  layer of white cotton; bottom
  layer of dark pink fabric
- Matching thread
- Embroidery scissors
- Thin needle
- Dressmaker's carbon paper
- Design (see p. 43)
- Pins
- Javana clear liner (acts in the
  same way as wax in batik
  work)
- Javana silk paint: green, violet,
  pink and azure blue
- Watercolour paintbrush
- Bowl with water
- Hairdryer
- Iron
- Masking-tape

Method

1. Cut the shape of the front piece of the dress out of the white and the dark pink material.

2. Tape the white material over the design which then will be visible through the material and trace the design with the Javana clear liner.

3. Dry the fabric with the hairdryer so as not to smudge the liner.

4. Carefully paint four well-diluted paints (blue, green, pink and violet) onto the material over the clear lines and allow them to flow together for a soft, delicate effect.

5. Dry the material again with a hairdryer.

6. Iron.

7. Tack the painted front piece of the dress onto the dark pink material along the outer edges and on both sides of the line which is going to be cut.

8. Cut along the resist line (see Photo 19).

9. Fold the cut edges under and sew them down onto the dark pink material.

10. Remove tacking stitches.

11. Tack the front piece of the dress onto the dress.

12. Turn the outer edges of the front piece under and sew onto the dress with small hemming stitches (Photo 19).

Photo 20: Seaside cushions
(Rita Vermeulen)

Two seaside cushions

Materials

- Two or three layers of material the top layer must be white cotton fabric
- Matching thread
- Embroidery scissors
- Thin needle
- Dressmaker's carbon paper
- Design (see pp. 44–45)
- Pins
- Javana silk paint - green
- Watercolour paintbrush
- Bowl with water
- Hairdryer
- Iron

Method

1. Paint the top layer of white cotton material with green Javana silk paint, allowing the colour to flow over the material. Add more water to the areas which need to be lighter in colour.

2. Dry with a hairdryer and then iron.

3. Tack the two or more layers of material together along the outer edges.

4. Place the dressmaker's carbon paper with the coloured side face down on the top layer of material. Put the design on top of the carbon and pin the design, carbon and material together. Trace the design onto the fabric with the ballpoint pen.

5. Remove the design and carbon paper.

6. The design consists of small islands. Tack the layers of material together between the islands 5 mm on the outside of the design lines.

7. Cut the islands out by piercing the top layer of the material with the point of the embroidery scissors and cutting 5 mm on the inside of the design lines. Cut only the top layer. Make incisions where necessary (Figs. 1–8 on page 7).

8. Fold the cut edges of the material under with the tip of the needle (Fig. 9 on page 7) and stitch them down onto the next layer with small hemming stitches.

9. Where there are more than two layers of material, draw a line 3 mm from the previous folded line with a marking pencil, cut 5 mm from this marked line, fold the edges under and sew down with small hemming stitches. Continue like this until the last layer of material is revealed.

10. Remove tacking stitches.

11. Appliqué eyes into position (Photo 20). On one cushion dotted material was used for the third layer.

San Blas painting

Photo 21: San Blas painting
(Marie Peacey)

Reject and overprinted scraps of material were used for the top layers to make these six pictures. Further detail, like the scales on the fish and the lines on the face, was embroidered with stem stitch (Photo 21).

Hand-stitching is most commonly used but a neat finish can also be obtained by stitching the cut edges down onto the next layer of material with a sewing machine, using satin stitch. This method is particularly suitable for place mats, bedspreads or clothing. Remember to use designs with wide curves for easy stitching.

Photo 22: Jacket with cut-away yoke (Jemima van Zyl)

Jacket

Materials

- White material for the jacket
- Royal blue material
- Printed material
- Matching thread
- Embroidery scissors
- Sewing machine
- Dressmaker's carbon paper
- Vilene
- Pins
- Design (see p. 46)

Method

1. Cut the yoke out of the royal blue and printed materials and tack together along the outer edges.

2. Trace the design onto thin Vilene.

3. Tack the Vilene under the wrong side of the printed material and also around the islands of the design.

4. Straight-stitch along the design line.

5. Turn over and cut out the islands by cutting through the royal blue material only so that the printed material is exposed. Keep close to the stitched line. Satin-stitch over the straight-stitched line.

6. Remove the Vilene.

7. Join the shoulder seams of the jacket and spread it open on a table.

8. Tack the yoke into position over the shoulders of the jacket.

9. Fold in the outer edges and stitch down onto the jacket with straight stitch close to the edge.

10. Sew up the underarm seams and finish the jacket (Photo 22).

Photo 23: Pink and blue cushions with machine-stitched cut-away (Nana van Eeden)

Pink and blue cushions
(two-layer cut-away with textured material)

Materials

- Chintz material
- Matching thread
- Sewing machine
- Embroidery scissors
- Thin needle
- Dressmaker's carbon paper
- Pins
- Design (see pp. 47–48)
- Matching bias binding

Method

1. Stitch small pin-tucks on one piece of material (Fig. 20).

2. Stitch wide tucks on another piece of material. Twist the wide tucks to one side and stitch down. Twist to the other side and stitch down again (Fig. 21).

3. Place the dressmaker's carbon paper with the coloured side face down on the top layer of material. Put the design on top of the carbon and pin the design, carbon and material together. Trace the design onto the material with the ballpoint pen.

4. Remove the design and carbon paper.

5. Tack the textured pieces of material under the top layer. Make sure that they correspond with the design on the top layer.

6. The design consists of small islands. Tack the layers of material together between the islands 5 mm on the outside of the design lines.

7. Cut the islands out by piercing the top layer of the material with the point of the embroidery scissors and cutting 5 mm on the inside of the design lines. Cut only the top layer. Make insicions where necessary (Figs. 1–8 on page 7).

8. Fold the cut edges of the material under with the tip of the needle (Fig. 9 on page 7), and stitch them down onto the next layer with small hemming stitches.

9. Remove the tacking stitches and complete the cushion covers, finishing them off with matching bias binding (Photo 23).

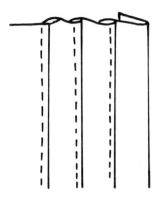

Fig. 20

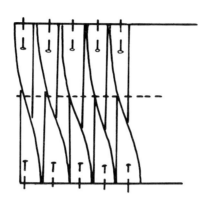

Fig. 21

Pattern 1: Cut-away decoration for a pocket (p. 5)

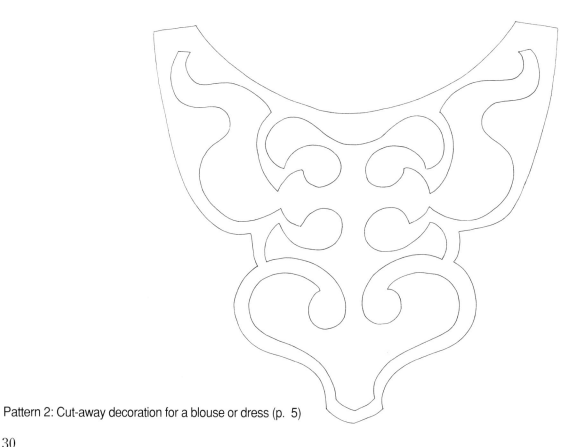

Pattern 2: Cut-away decoration for a blouse or dress (p. 5)

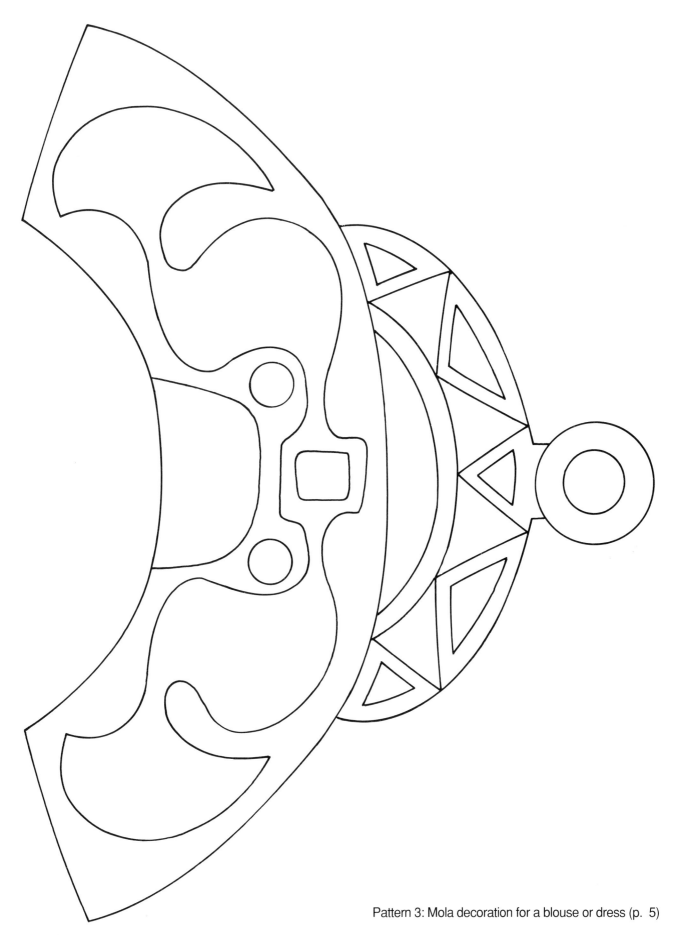

Pattern 3: Mola decoration for a blouse or dress (p. 5)

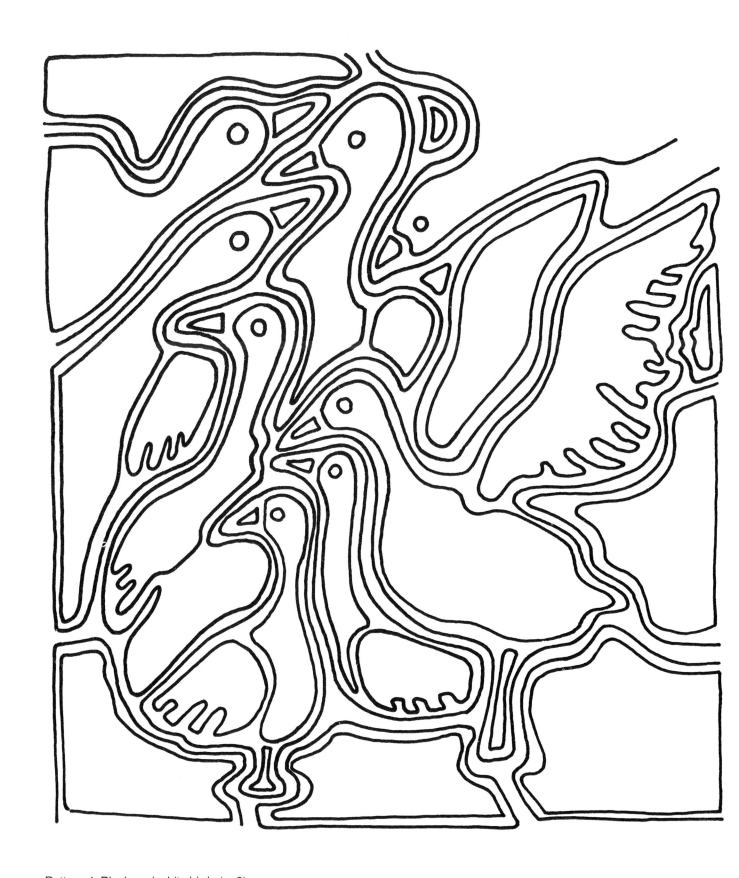

Pattern 4: Black-and-white birds (p. 9)

Pattern 5: Thin-line appliqué (p. 12)

Pattern 6: Basque for harem pants (p. 13)

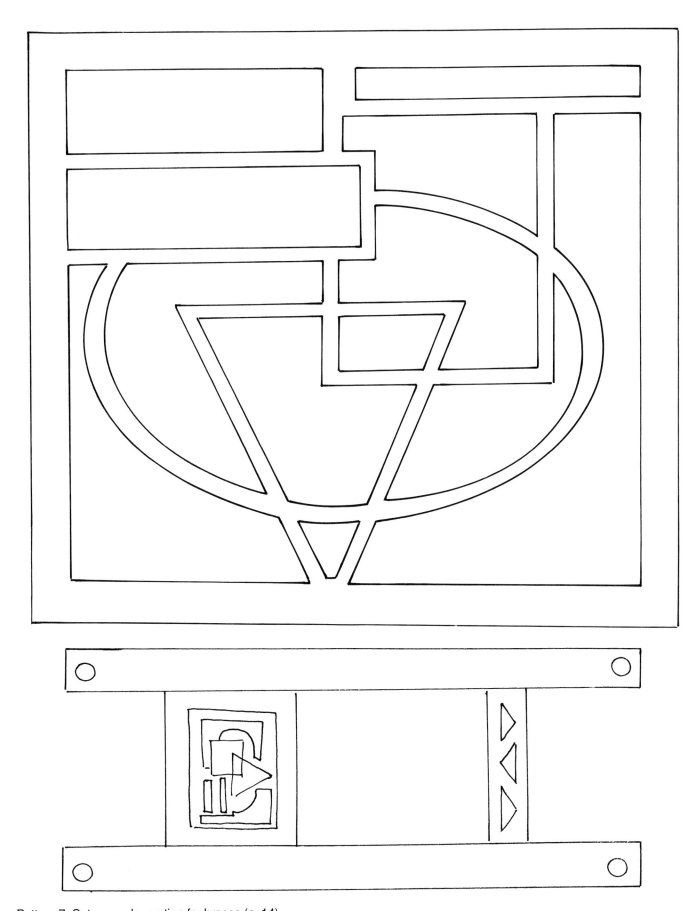

Pattern 7: Cut-away decoration for braces (p. 14)

Pattern 8: Tea cosy (p. 15)

Pattern 9: Decoration on a purple waistcoat (p. 15)

Pattern 10: Decoration on a jacket (p. 16)

Pattern 11: Decoration on a T-shirt (p. 17)

Pattern 12: Cut-away decoration for a jacket collar (p. 17)

Pattern 13: Belt (p. 20)

Pattern 14: White face (p. 21)

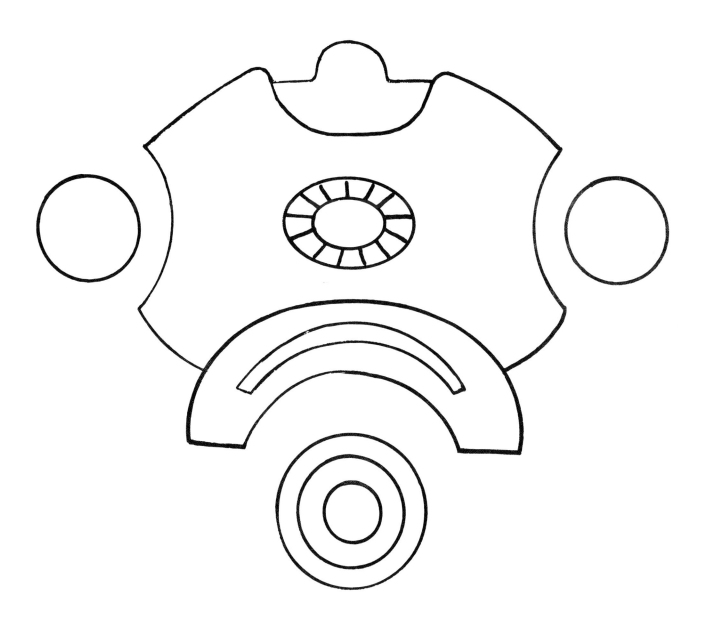

Pattern 15: Cut-away decoration for a knitted garment (p. 22)

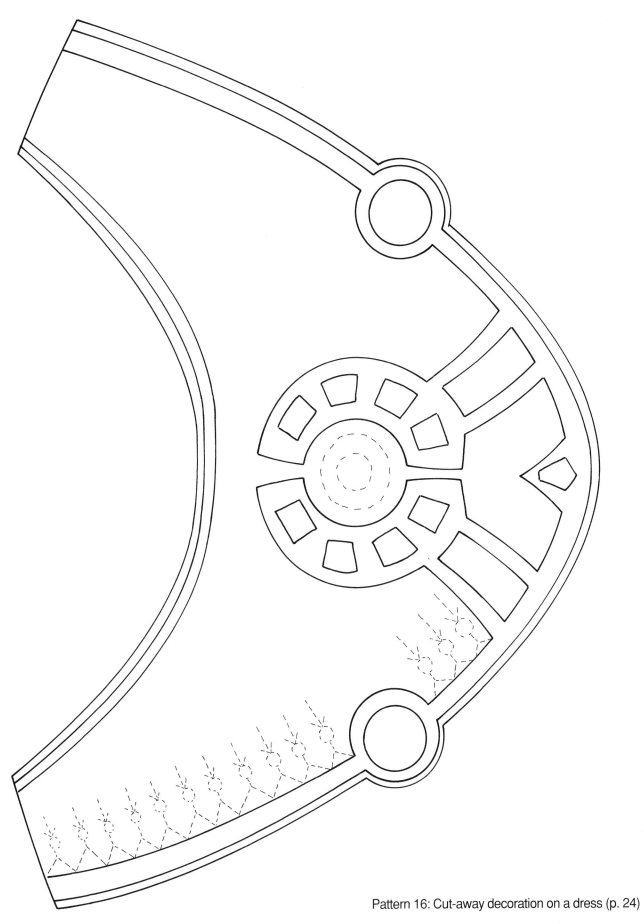

Pattern 16: Cut-away decoration on a dress (p. 24)

Pattern 17: Fish on a cushion cover (p. 25)

Pattern 18: Sea horse on a cushion cover (p. 25)

Pattern 19: Cut-away yoke for a jacket (p. 27)

Pattern 20: Cushion cover with machine-stitched cut-away (p. 28)

Pattern 21: Cushion cover with machine-stitched cut-away (p. 28)